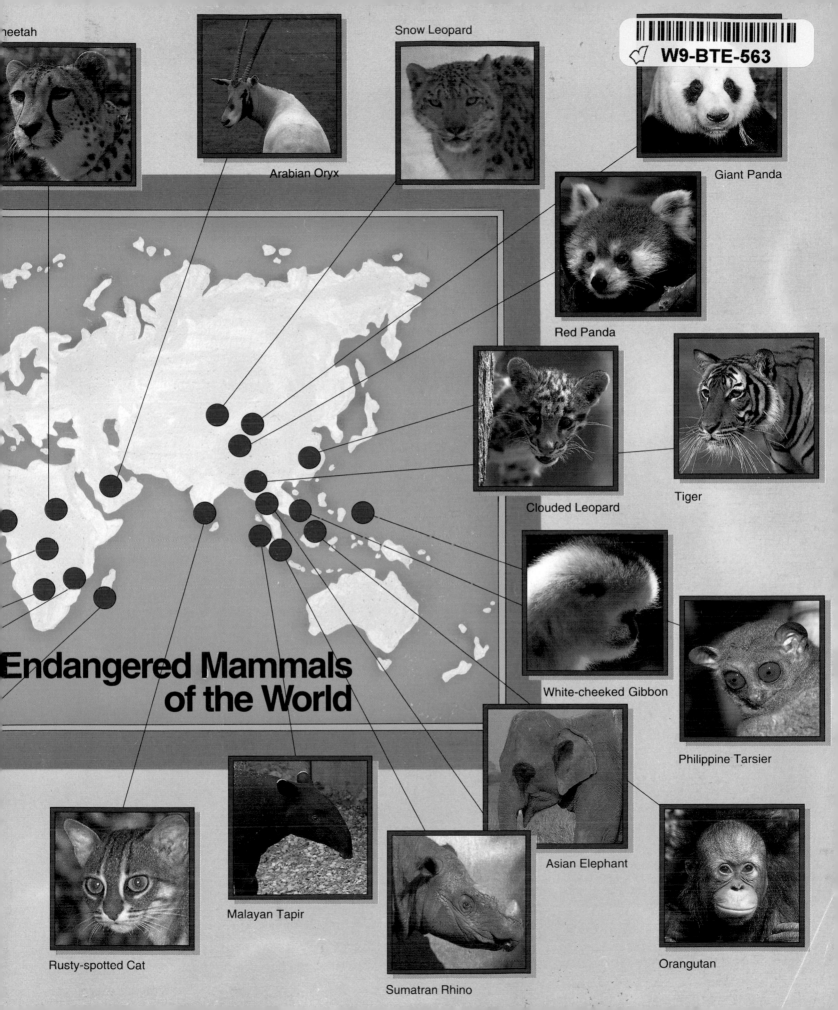

Cheetah

Arabian Oryx

Snow Leopard

Giant Panda

Red Panda

Clouded Leopard

Tiger

White-cheeked Gibbon

Philippine Tarsier

Endangered Mammals
of the World

Rusty-spotted Cat

Malayan Tapir

Sumatran Rhino

Asian Elephant

Orangutan

SAVING ENDANGERED MAMMALS

A FIELD GUIDE TO SOME OF THE EARTH'S RAREST ANIMALS

BY THANE MAYNARD

A Cincinnati Zoo Book

FRANKLIN WATTS

New York • Chicago • London • Toronto • Sydney

**This book is dedicated to Caitlin, Shailah, and Lily—and all of tomorrow's conservationists:
May you have the good sense to live as if the future matters.**

Frontis: Female white-cheeked gibbon

All photographs copyright © Cincinnati Zoo/Ron Austing except: U.S. Fish and Wildlife Service: pp. 13 top (Luther Goldman), 13 bottom (Rick Krueger), 54 top (George Harrison), 54 center (Ronald Bell), 54 bottom (Robin Hunter); Kathleen Stewart: p. 47.

Library of Congress Cataloging-in-Publication Data

Maynard, Thane.
Saving endangered mammals : a field guide to some of the earth's
rarest animals / by Thane Maynard.
p.   cm. — (A Cincinnati zoo book)
Includes bibliographical references and index.
Summary: Includes basic facts about a number of endangered mammals
and gives information on the threats they face and on efforts to
save them from extinction.
ISBN 0-531-15253-7 (Trade)   ISBN 0-531-11076-1 (Library)
1. Rare mammals—Juvenile literature. 2. Endangered species—
Juvenile literature. 3. Wildlife conservation—Juvenile
literature. [1. Rare animals. 2. Mammals. 3. Wildlife
conservation.] I. Title. II. Series.
QL706.8.M38 1992
599'.0042—dc20   92-14439
                                                                                        CIP AC

WHAT IS AN ENDANGERED SPECIES?

An endangered species is a type of plant or animal whose **population** has become so small that it is in danger of becoming **extinct**, or dying off forever.

WHY ARE MAMMALS ENDANGERED?

DESTRUCTION OF HABITAT is the biggest problem for wildlife today. This affects species such as jaguars, tigers, monkeys, and apes.

POACHING, or illegal hunting, affects mammals such as elephants, rhinos, and all the spotted cats.

POLLUTION kills aquatic animals, insects, and predatory birds. Loss of these species affects mammals who feed on them.

TRADE IN EXOTIC PETS directly affects the wild populations of a wide variety of monkeys and cats. Exotic-pet dealers also provide wolves, kangaroos, and even bears for people's homes.

HUMAN POPULATION GROWTH and poorly planned development squeeze out many species, including the Giant Panda, from their native habitat.

OVERFISHING, OVERHUNTING AND COMMERCIAL PRESSURE can lead to the killing of too many of some animals, such as whales and porpoises. The population may fall to dangerously low levels.

WHAT IS BEING DONE
TO SAVE ENDANGERED MAMMALS?

Scientists and conservation groups are working on laws to protect wildlife. But they need assistance and, all over the world, people are trying to help. School children are replanting a huge forest in Costa Rica. In the United States, students are collecting and recycling paper, plastics, and other materials, and working for energy-saving programs. Wildlife conservation is more than just saving wild plants and animals; it is about saving ourselves, because human beings share the fate of all Earth's inhabitants. To save the wild species of our planet we need:

- **Species and ecosystem research**
- **Identification of critical habitats**
- **Establishment of preserves and protection of habitats**
- **Technical training for future conservationists**
- **Conservation education**
- **Stronger environmental preservation laws**
- **Conservation of natural resources**

Saving Endangered Mammals provides descriptions, photographs and range maps of 25 mammals that are at risk and tells what is being done to save some of them. None of these species are safe from extinction yet, but some are making a comeback—as the result of the work of researchers, native peoples and conservationists. With the information here, and the list of conservation groups on page 56, every reader can join the efforts to save these wonderful creatures.

African Elephant

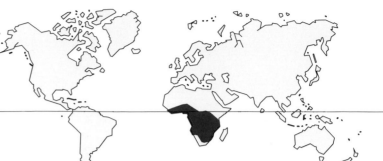

Loxodonta africana

Range: Africa, south of the Sahara Desert
Size: Shoulder height: 8–13 ft (2.43–3.96 m)
Weight: 5,000–13,000 lbs (2,250–5,850 kg)
Habitat: Forested savanna
Food: Grasses, bark, trees, shrubs, roots
Reproduction: Gestation: nearly 2 years; one calf every 3–5 years
Life Span: 60–70 years in captivity
Threats: Poaching, loss of habitat

African elephants are the largest land animals on Earth. In addition to having the biggest teeth, noses, and feet of any land animal, elephants also have the biggest ears. The ears are not used just for hearing though; they also serve as heat dispersers. As they flap, the blood that circulates close to the surface on the back of the ears is cooled.

Ancestors of elephants—mammoths and mastodons—once ranged over much of the world. Now, because of rapidly growing human population, the African elephant is confined to ever-shrinking areas in Africa. One reason for the elephant's decreasing numbers is the value poachers find in its ivory tusks. The tusks are actually elongated incisor teeth used for digging and for sparring between males.

Today there are still about 600,000 African elephants alive in the wild. That may sound like a lot, but there were more than twice that number in 1980! Most were illegally killed by poachers, as wholesale ivory prices reached an all-time high of $100 a pound on the black market. A worldwide ban on ivory sales was begun in 1990 to help stop the killing of elephants.

More than trade in their teeth is killing elephants. About 700 million people live in Africa today, and scientists predict there will be twice as many by the year 2014. All those people need food and places to live, so there will be less and less space for elephants. In agricultural areas elephants are always driven out, since a herd of elephants can eat a farmer's entire crop in a single night.

Arabian Oryx

Oryx leucoryx

Range: Formerly, Middle East, reintroduced into Oman and Jordan
Size: Shoulder height: 3–4 ft (.91–1.21 m)
Weight: 143–165 lbs (64.86–74.85 kg)
Habitat: Stony desert and semi-arid lands
Food: Short, sparse desert grasses
Reproduction: Gestation: 6 months; one calf per year
Life Span: 15–20 years
Threats: Warfare, poaching

Everything about the Arabian oryx, a type of antelope, suits it to the climate extremes of the desert. Its small size reduces its food and water needs and its white coat helps it avoid overheating. The Arabian oryx is able to survive in the desert by eating the sparse desert grasses.

The desert supports few **predators**, so the Arabian oryx has developed no natural defense against human hunters except to run. It was hunted so heavily in the mid-twentieth century that by 1970 it was extinct in the wild. Conservationists made a desperate attempt in the 1960s to rescue the last remaining animals. Two males and a female were caught and sent to the Phoenix Zoo in Arizona, chosen because its climate best suited these desert animals. They formed the core of what became known as the World Herd.

A species cannot be maintained with just three founding animals, so requests were sent out to all zoos holding oryx. Animals were sent from the London Zoo in England and the Riyadh Zoo in Saudi Arabia, bringing the World Herd up to nine. These founders were carefully paired for breeding to produce genetically strong and healthy offspring to be returned to the wild. Such planning prevents inbreeding and is essential in a reintroduction program, because unplanned breeding may favor adaptation to captive living over traits needed to survive in the wild.

The herd soon grew large enough to be divided among other zoos. Several animals were released to a newly formed reserve in Jordan, and later to another in Oman. Their success led to additional oryx being sent to zoos around the world, including the Cincinnati Zoo, with the understanding that offspring will be made available for release to the wild as needed.

Asian Elephant

Elephas maximus

Range: India, Nepal, Indochina, Malaysia, Indonesia, South China
Size: Shoulder height: 8.2–9.8 ft (2.5–3 m)
Weight: 8,000–11,000 lbs (3,600–5,000 kg)
Habitat: Forest
Food: Bamboo, grasses, leaves, bark, trees, shrubs
Life Span: 60 years in captivity
Reproduction: Gestation: 22 months; one calf every 3–5 years
Threats: Poaching, loss of habitat

The Asian elephant is usually smaller than its African cousin, and has considerably smaller ears. It also has smoother skin and less prominent tusks. Asian elephants live in large family groups called herds and feed entirely on the forest plants. A single elephant may eat hundreds of pounds of food per day, bringing it all up to its mouth with its famous and unusual appendage, the trunk—an organ formed from its nose and upper lip.

Without its trunk, the elephant could not survive. Besides carrying food and water to its mouth, the trunk is used for breathing, and for spraying the elephant's back with dust or water to protect it from the sun. Elephants have even been known to use their trunks as snorkels while swimming or walking under water.

The trunk of an elephant has no bones, yet is one of the strongest appendages possessed by any animal. Using more than 30,000 interconnecting muscles and tendons, the trunk is strong enough to pick up giant logs and drag them through the forest, yet is so sensitive it can pick up a coin or peanut from the ground.

The Asian elephant once ranged from Mesopotamia (in the region now known as Iraq) throughout Asia south of the Himalayas all the way to Northern China. Today, Asian elephants are found scattered only in isolated pockets of India, Nepal, Sumatra, and Southern Asia.

For centuries the Asian elephant has been overhunted for its ivory tusks that are used for carvings and jewelry. Today, Asian elephants are in even greater danger of extinction because of loss of their natural habitat. Only an estimated 30,000 to 50,000 still remain in the wild.

Black Rhinoceros

Diceros bicornis

Range: Protected areas in eastern and southern Africa
Size: Shoulder height: 4.5–5 ft (1.37–1.52 m)
Weight: 2,000–4,000 lbs (900–1,800 kg)
Habitat: Grassland, bush, forest
Food: Shrubs, grass, herbs, acacia twigs and leaves
Reproduction: Gestation: 15 months; one calf every 2–4 years
Life Span: 35–40 years
Threats: Poaching, loss of habitat, low reproduction rates

The black rhinoceros, a solitary vegetarian, travels along browsing on leaves and twigs. Its two horns are not made of bone, as are the horns of most animals. Instead, they are made of fibers that are like matted hair, which grow as much as 3 inches (7.62 cm) a year throughout the rhino's life. While their purpose is protection, the valuable horns often lead to death at the hands of greedy poachers.

African rhinos were heavily depleted by European hunters in the 1800s. Since 1970, the black rhino population has decreased from 70,000 to less than 3,000 in 1992, as prices for rhino horn have skyrocketed and agriculture has transformed their habitat.

As long as demand remains high for rhino horn, little will deter armed poachers. Today illegally traded rhinoceros horn is, ounce for ounce, more valuable than gold. There are two major markets for the horn: pharmaceutical companies in the Far East that manufacture a wide variety of products from beer to medicines and elixirs; and people who wish to sport daggers with rare rhino horn handles.

In the African country of Namibia, wildlife officials are sawing off the horns of rhinos to remove the poachers' incentive to kill the animals. Rhinos can survive without their horns. Unfortunately, since the extremely elusive rhinos often hide in thick bush, and poachers generally hunt under cover of darkness, the lack of horn is often not noticed until it's too late.

Black-footed Ferret

Mustela nigripes

Range: Formerly, western prairies of North America
Size: 21 in (53.3 cm), including tail
Weight: 1.2–2 lbs (.54–.91 kg)
Habitat: Western prairies; within range of prairie dogs
Food: Prairie dogs and other small mammals
Reproduction: Gestation: 42–45 days; litter: 3–4
Life Span: 10–12 years
Threats: Poisoning of prey; currently, dangerously low population

The black-footed ferret is a slender-bodied weasel with yellowish fur and black feet, face mask, and tail tip. It is similar in appearance to the European domestic ferret, which is popular as a pet. Both animals, like all weasels, are excellent rodent hunters. In fact, the term "to ferret out" derives from their ability to tunnel through rodent or rabbit burrows chasing prey.

The black-footed ferret is one of the most endangered animals in the world and the single most endangered mammal in North America. It was originally found only within the range of the prairie dog, its main food source, on the Great Plains of western North America. Today there are no known populations of black-footed ferrets in the wild. Once only 18 animals remained, but thanks to captive breeding, over 300 ferrets were alive in 1992.

The decline in the population of the black-footed ferret is an indirect result of the advance of agriculture across the western United States and Canada. Plowing up natural prairie to grow crops has greatly reduced prairie dog habitat; and the farmers' practice of poisoning prairie dogs has been less effective on the prairie dogs they consider pests than on the black-footed ferret. Prairie dogs are rodents that can bounce back quickly from a population decline, but ferrets are predators with a naturally low population spread over a broad range. As the number of ferrets declined it became more and more difficult for the animals to replenish themselves.

The U.S. Fish and Wildlife Service has established a recovery plan for the black-footed ferret. It is working to get the captive ferret population up to a level where they can begin to be reintroduced to the wild. The ultimate goal of the program is to create 10 separate wild ferret populations, totaling 1,500 animals, by the end of the twentieth century.

Cheetah

Acinonyx jubatus

Range: Africa, formerly South Asia and Middle East
Size: 30–36 in (76.2–91.44 cm)
Weight: 86–143 lbs (39–64.86 kg)
Habitat: Most habitats in Africa except rain forest
Food: Gazelles, impala, wildebeest calves and other hoofed mammals up to their own weight; also hares in some areas
Reproduction: Gestation: 91–95 days; litter: 1–5 cubs
Life Span: Up to 12 years; 17 years in captivity
Threats: Habitat loss, poaching

Cheetahs are the fastest land animal, able to reach speeds up to 70 miles an hour (112.6 kph) when chasing gazelles and other antelopes—their favorite foods. Cheetahs, unlike other cats, have nonretractile claws. Their claws work like cleats on track shoes, to provide traction. But it takes more than fancy footwear to run so fast. Cheetahs have incredibly flexible spines that work like springs to add extra thrust. As a result, they can take a dozen strides per second, and accelerate from zero to 60 miles per hour (96.5 kph) in three seconds! Scientists estimate that if horses had such flexible backbones they could run 100 miles per hour (160.9 kph).

With all this tremendous speed, the cheetah is a sprinter, not a long-distance runner. If the chase for food is longer than 300 yards (274.32 m), a cheetah becomes winded and badly needs a rest.

Cheetahs were once numerous across Africa, Asia, and the Middle East. Today they are considered endangered in Africa and probably extinct in most of their Asian and Middle Eastern range. The fur trade, habitat loss, and the animal's persecution as a pest have led to its decline. In the late 1960s, as many as 5,000 cheetah skins were brought into the United States each year, to be made into coats, shoes, and handbags. Fortunately, today that trade has stopped.

Cheetahs are fast, but they can't outrun extinction without help. Conservationists are working to save the cheetah in Africa by protecting national parks and wildlife refuges from encroachment by farmers and hunters. In zoos, scientists are studying cheetah genetics to help in their captive breeding. Through blood tests, skin grafts and DNA research, it has been discovered that all cheetahs are closely related, in the wild as well as in zoos. No one is certain why this is, but it is thought that cheetahs nearly became extinct thousands of years ago and that all present-day cheetahs may be the descendants of a single population that survived.

Clouded Leopard

Neofelis nebulosa

Range: India, South China, Nepal, Burma, Indochina to Sumatra and Borneo
Size: Shoulder height: About 20 in (50.8 cm)
Weight: 30–70 lbs (13.61–31.75 kg)
Habitat: Dense forest at altitudes up to 6,570 ft (2,000 m)
Food: Monkeys, squirrels, birds, and other small animals
Reproduction: Gestation: 85–90 days; 2–4 cubs
Life Span: Up to 17 years in captivity
Threats: Poaching, habitat loss

The clouded leopard is about the size of a medium-sized dog. It has a long body, relatively short legs, and a tail that can be equal in length to its head and body combined. This cat's coat is unique, ranging from dark brown to yellow, marked with elongated, irregular, cloudy blotches of darker shades, making it one of the most beautiful cats in the world. Its very thick tail is encircled with black rings.

Because of its large upper teeth, which are relatively longer than in any other cat species, the clouded leopard is sometimes referred to as a "modern day sabretooth." In Malay this cat is called *rimaudahan*, which means "tree tiger," a name derived from its habits of sleeping in trees as well as laying in wait in the branches, watching for prey to pass by.

The clouded leopard has been hunted for its beautiful fur for many years, and it takes from 20 to 30 cats to make one full-length coat! Fortunately, an international agreement called CITES, or the Convention on International Trade of Endangered Species, makes it illegal to buy or sell products made from endangered animals and plants. This protects the clouded leopard and hundreds of other species.

As a result, poaching is not the clouded leopard's biggest threat. They are rain forest creatures and depend upon the forest and its intricate web of plants and animals for survival. As the jungles are destroyed, so are the clouded leopards. But saving the rain forests isn't important just to save leopards, parrots, and pythons. It's really about saving ourselves. Because as the forests go, so do we.

Cotton-top Tamarin

Saguinus oedipus

Range: Northwestern Colombia
Size: 6–10 in (15.24–23.40 cm) long, plus long tail
Weight: 1–2 lbs (.45–.91 kg)
Habitat: Tropical rain forests
Food: Fruit, sap, insects, bird eggs, small animals
Life Span: 12–15 years in captivity, less in the wild
Reproduction: Gestation: 164 days; almost always bears twins
Main Threat: Deforestation

Tamarins like the cotton-top, and their cousins the marmosets, are the smallest monkeys in the world. All tamarins and marmosets live in the forests of tropical Central and South America.

In cotton-top tamarin society, everyone contributes to rearing the young. Both parents take care of the babies, and even the older siblings share the responsibilities. In fact, behavioral researchers have observed that cotton-top tamarins need the experience of raising young because their parenting behavior is learned, unlike the instinctive behavior of cats and dogs.

Of course, there is a reason for the communal care. Cotton-top tamarins almost always have twins, and the babies' combined weight is 15 percent of their mother's weight. That is the equivalent of a human mother having twin 10-pound (4.54-kg) babies. If you're wondering how these little monkeys hold onto their babies while they are climbing through the treetops, the answer is that they don't. The babies hold onto the fur of the older tamarins while hitching a ride on their backs.

Today the cotton-top tamarin is restricted to a series of isolated forest patches in northwestern Colombia. It is estimated that there are fewer than 2,500 left in the wild, and that number continues to decline. More than 2,000 square miles (5,180 sq km) of rain forest are destroyed every year, in Colombia alone. That is an area the size of the state of Delaware.

Scientists are studying the cotton-top tamarin's behavior and physiology in order to help protect the species. And Colombian conservationists and school children are working together on a program called *Proyecto Tití*, which means "Project Tamarin." Its aim is to teach people living in and near the rain forest that both monkeys and humans depend upon the forest for survival.

Giant Panda

Ailuropoda melanoleuca

Range: Szechuan, Shensi, and Kansu provinces of central and western China.
Size: Shoulder height: 27–32 in (68.58–81.28 cm)
Weight: 220–330 pounds (99.7–149.5 kg)
Habitat: Cool, damp bamboo forests at altitudes of 8,500–11,500 ft (2,590.8–3,505.2 m)
Food: Bamboo leaves and stems, bulbs, grasses, small animals
Reproduction: Gestation: 125–150 days; can bear 1–3 young, but only one can be reared
Life Span: Unknown in the wild; over 20 years in captivity
Threats: Habitat destruction and food loss

Scientists have long debated how to classify the giant panda. Many thought it was a bear; others placed the panda in a separate category with its cousin, the red panda, between the bear and the raccoon. Today, most taxonomists (scientists who classify animals) group the giant panda with the bears of the world.

Giant pandas live in the cold, damp bamboo forests at high altitudes in China, but contrary to legend, they do not feed solely on bamboo. Like other bears, pandas are partially omnivorous, feeding on both plants and animals. Pandas will sometimes spend 10 to 12 hours a day searching for and eating food. While the mainstay of their diet is bamboo and their future depends upon the survival of the bamboo forests, pandas also eat some other grasses, flowers, and small animals.

The pandas are well-equipped to manage their bamboo diet. Their huge heads have powerful jaw muscles that enable them to eat the plant—one of the toughest in the world. While it is actually a type of grass, bamboo is harder to chew than plywood, making it impossible for most animals, including ourselves, to eat.

One of the most recognizable and well-loved animals on Earth, the giant panda has been used as a symbol of wildlife conservation by the World Wildlife Fund since that organization began in 1961. Today fewer than 800 pandas remain in the wild. It takes more than affection to save wild species, and if the panda is to survive, it needs help from the people of China. All over the world, wherever endangered species are making comebacks, it is as a result of wildlife laws and the protection of wild areas. With over a billion people in China today, it is hard to protect wildlife habitats. But if the Chinese support the effort, they will save the panda.

Gorilla

Gorilla gorilla

Range: Central Africa
Size of Animal: Height: 5.6–5.9 ft (1.71–1.80 m)
Weight: 200–600 lbs (90.72–272.16 kg)
Habitat: Tropical forest
Food: Leaves, stems, herbs, shrubs, vines
Reproduction: Gestation: 250–270 days; usually single births
Life Span: 35 years in the wild; 50 years in captivity
Threats: Poaching, deforestation

The gorilla is the largest living primate, weighing up to 600 pounds (272.16 kg). But not all gorillas are such giants; the males are generally twice as large as the females.

There are three sub-species, or races, of gorillas: eastern and western lowland gorillas and mountain gorillas. No zoos have mountain gorillas in their collections. The gorillas you see in zoos are western lowland gorillas. What separates western from eastern lowland gorillas is the Zaire River, formerly called the Congo. The river creates a barrier because unlike people, gorillas don't swim. Mountain gorillas live in the African countries of Rwanda, Uganda and Zaire. They have longer hair than the lowland gorillas, especially on the arms, and are the most endangered.

Contrary to the belief that they are ferocious creatures, gorillas are actually very gentle and docile. Scientists studying their behavior often get as close as several meters. The only time gorillas are aggressive is when they are protecting their family groups. These groups often consist of one fully adult male called the silverback, five to ten females that the male protects, and their offspring. The silverback plays a very important role in the group, not only as protector, but also as the central link among the females. Young females leave their family when they mature, so all the adult females in a group are unrelated. It is each female's tie to the silverback that keeps the group together.

Many tourists visit Africa hoping to glimpse live wild gorillas. This new kind of eco-tourism promotes experiences in the wild and produces greater profit than poaching, so gorillas are starting to receive more protection. In 1991 tourists spent more than a million dollars to see the mountain gorillas in Virunga National Park in Rwanda. As a result, local people are now involved in protecting the gorillas and their habitat because they realize that without the forest, there would be no gorillas, and without the gorillas, there would be no tourists.

Gray Wolf

Canis lupus

Range: North America, Europe, Asia, and the Middle East
Size: Shoulder height: 26–32 in (66.04–81.28 cm)
Weight: 27–175 lbs (12.25–79.38 kg)
Habitat: Forests, taiga, tundra, deserts, plains and mountains
Food: Moose, deer, caribou, and smaller animals; some plant material in season
Reproduction: Gestation: 61–63 days; litter: 4–7 pups
Life Span: 8–16 years; up to 20 years in captivity
Threats: Poaching, loss of food supply due to human hunting

The gray wolf is a large canine that resembles the Alaskan malamute, a domestic dog, in appearance. Adult males average nearly 100 pounds (45.36 kg), but some weigh as much as 175 pounds (79.38 kg)! However, it isn't just their size that enables them to hunt animals as large as elk and moose—it is their family structure, the pack. The gray wolf is a social animal that lives in a pack, or family group, of as many as 20 animals. The average pack size is 7 or 8 animals. A wolf pack is highly organized and disciplined, with a very high degree of cooperation used in hunting and breeding. Wolves can run for hours at a time, so by coordinating and sustaining their attacks they are able to kill animals much bigger and faster than themselves.

For centuries some humans have been fearful of wolves. But the popular image that wolves eat human beings is an exaggeration. Wolves do not hunt people; they prefer hoofed animals such as deer, elk, and moose. Today most people realize this, but western ranchers are still concerned because wolves will also sometimes kill livestock. Fortunately, more and more people are learning that there is room for both wolves and ranching to coexist. In Minnesota and Montana, funds have been established to compensate ranchers for livestock losses caused by wolves. If a problem from a certain wolf or pack persists, the U.S. Fish and Wildlife Service will relocate or sometimes kill the wolves.

Conservationists hope to reintroduce the gray wolf into Yellowstone National Park in Wyoming.

Jaguar

Panthera onca

Range: Southwestern United States to Central Patagonia
Size: Shoulder height: 32–38 in (81.28–96.52 cm)
Weight: 125–250 lbs (56.7–113.4 kg)
Habitat: Tropical forests, swamps, open country
Food: Peccary, deer, monkeys, tapir, sloths, birds, caimans
Reproduction: Gestation: 93–110 days; Litter: 2–4
Life Span: Up to 20 years in captivity
Threats: Poaching, habitat loss

The jaguar has been culturally and historically important to the Indians of South America as a symbol of royalty. It is the largest cat of the Western Hemisphere, and the largest spotted cat in the world. It is heavier and has a more massive chest than its old world relative, the leopard. The jaguar's coat is dark gray in color, as seen here, or tawny, with black spots.

To us, a jaguar's spots are beautiful; but for jaguars, the spots are camouflage, helping them to blend in among the vegetation as they hunt at night. If you confuse the leopard and the jaguar, look for the donut-shaped rings *with the spots inside* to "spot" the jaguar.

Even though jaguars are thought of as tropical rain forest cats, they also live in more open areas. Like all cats, they are strictly **carnivores**, hunting a wide variety of **prey** in order to survive. They can be nearly as large as a female African lion and can kill very large prey, including animals bigger than themselves, such as tapir and deer.

Although they once lived from Texas to below the equator in South America, jaguars are decreasing in number throughout much of their range because of habitat loss and hunting. But they are also a modern-day conservation success story.

The small Central American country of Belize has established the world's first jaguar refuge, a 102,000-acre (41,279-ha) park called the Cockscomb Basin Jaguar Preserve. It was created as the result of Belizian scientists, government officials, and people living in and near the preserve working together to help save an important wild area for the future. The park is a huge piece of land in such a small country. It would be similar to the United States setting aside the entire state of Missouri as a wildlife refuge.

Malayan Tapir

Tapirus indicus

Range: Burma, Thailand, Malay Peninsula, Sumatra
Size: Shoulder height: 34–42 in (86.36–106.68 cm)
Weight: 550–660 lbs (249.48–299.38 kg)
Habitat: Dense primary rain forests
Food: Grasses, aquatic vegetation, leaves, buds, twigs, fruits of low-growing shrubs
Reproduction: Gestation: 390–395 days; a female can produce one infant every 18 months
Life Span: 30 years
Main Threat: Deforestation, poaching

The tapir is actually related to the horse and to the rhinoceros, though it looks something like a cross between a pig and an elephant. Its extended snout is used for reaching leaves and for smelling food and nearby predators. Tapirs are shy animals; they are quick to flee, and generally live alone or in pairs.

When the young are small they have vivid stripes and spots that help them to blend into the thick underbrush of their forest home.

Malayan tapirs live in tropical forests and spend much of their time in and near the water, even wallowing in the mud. They are mostly nocturnal, feeding at night.

Today there are four species of tapir. The Malayan tapir lives in the jungles of Southeast Asia and Malaysia; in Central and South America there are three separate kinds of tapir. The Central American, or Baird's, tapir lives in the Central American countries of Belize, Guatemala, and southern Mexico. The mountain tapir lives in the Andes, at an elevation of 14,000 feet (4267 m). And the lowland, or Brazilian, tapir ranges from Colombia to Brazil. Fossil records suggest that there were once many more species of tapir distributed throughout the world. Some species may date back almost 50 million years.

Like most animals of the tropical rain forest, the Malayan tapir is suffering from habitat loss. As the Southeast Asian and the Malaysian forests are cleared for timber and agriculture, the tapir is left with no place to live. And what forest still remains offers them fewer places to hide, leaving them more susceptible to predators and to poaching.

Okapi

Okapia johnstoni

Range: Northern and northeastern Zaire
Size: Shoulder height: 5–6 ft (1.52–1.82 m)
Weight: 465–660 lbs (210.93–299.38 kg)
Habitat: Dense rain forest
Food: Leaves and young shoots of trees, seeds, fruits
Reproduction: Gestation: 14–15 months; one calf every 2–3 years
Life Span: 15 years
Threats: Tropical deforestation, poaching

One of the last large mammals to be "discovered," the okapi was not known to scientists until the late nineteenth century, when it was observed by the British explorer and author, Sir Harry Johnston. The only living relative of the giraffe, this rare and secretive animal's shorter neck and legs allow it to slip easily through the forest, avoiding detection by leopards and humans, its natural predators. The okapi is also called the forest giraffe.

The most striking similarity between the okapi and the giraffe is the long, prehensile tongue. It is used for pulling leaves off branches, as well as for grooming hard-to-reach places. The okapi can even clean its ears with its tongue!

The okapi's dark color and striped markings, combined with its acute hearing and great speed, make it hard to spot in the forest. It is a solitary animal, coming together only for mating. This elusiveness protects it from hunters, but it also makes it difficult for researchers to study its behavior and keep track of its numbers. This knowledge is essential if we are to protect this rare and beautiful animal from eventual extinction.

The Ituri Forest of Zaire (formerly called the Congo) is the native home of the okapi. It is also the home of the Pygmy tribes who gave this animal its name: *O'api.* A dense, dark jungle, the Ituri Forest protects many other elusive animals only recently discovered, such as the pygmy chimpanzee and the Congo peacock, Africa's only pheasant.

Like all inhabitants of the Ituri Forest, the okapi's future depends on the survival of the forest itself, which is threatened by the growing human population around it. If the forest is cut down and destroyed, the okapi will live only as a relic in zoos around the world.

Orangutan

Pongo pygmaeus

Range: Northern Sumatra, most of lowland Borneo
Size: Height: 45–54 in (114.3–137.16 cm)
Weight: 88–200 lbs (39.92–90.72 kg)
Habitat: Lowland and tropical hill rain forest
Food: Fruits, young leaves, insects, tree bark
Reproduction: Gestation: 260–270 days; usually one baby per birth
Life Span: Up to 35 years; up to 50 years in captivity
Threats: Deforestation, poaching

The orangutan is strictly a tropical forest animal. In fact, in Malaysia the name orangutan means "Person of the Forest." With long arms well suited for climbing, orangutans are **arboreal**, spending most of their time up in trees, either sleeping or foraging. At night they will often form a "nest" for sleeping 30 to 70 feet (9.14 to 21.33 m) above the ground. The nest is constructed of branches and leaves, and must be strong since orangutans can be as large as humans. But the animal may move on the next day in search of plants to eat, and build a new nest the following night. Unlike gorillas and chimpanzees—whose social behavior is well known— orangutans tend to live more solitary lives. Mothers with young will often travel together, but adult males usually live alone.

There are two separate sub-species of orangutan; one lives in the lowland forests of Borneo and the other in northern Sumatra. There are some differences in appearance between the two groups, which are most noticeable in the males. An adult male Bornean orangutan has an enormous face, complete with giant cheek flanges and a huge dewlap, or throat sac. The Sumatran orangutan is slimmer and lighter colored, with a longer face and a red moustache which make it appear much more humanlike than its Bornean cousin. Youngsters of both races have a blue tinge to their faces.

For nearly 20 years orangutans have been studied in the wild by Dr. Birute Galdikas. Most of what is known of orangutan behavior has been learned from the research she and a number of other scientists have conducted in the forests of Indonesia. Unfortunately, they have also documented that as the forests are cleared for agriculture and timber, this solitary animal is being crowded out of existence. Pet trade is also responsible for the removal of many young orangs from the wild.

Philippine Tarsier

Tarsius syrichta

Range: Southeastern Philippine Islands
(Samar, Mindanao)
Size: Length: 8.3–10 in (20.75–25.4 cm), including tail
Weight: 3.9–4.2 oz (110.57–119.07 g)
Habitat: Rain forest and shrub
Food: Many kinds of arthropods; ants, beetles,
cockroaches, scorpions, and small animals
Reproduction: Gestation: about 6 months; single young is born
Life Span: 8–12 years in captivity
Threats: Logging; loss of habitat to agriculture

The Philippine tarsier seems built for life in the trees. Weighing only about 3 to 4 ounces (113 g), it is one of the smallest primates in the world. Tarsiers are noted for their leaping ability; they use their froglike hind legs to spring from branch to branch, often as far as 6 feet (1.82 m) in one leap. Unlike many of the higher primates—the monkeys and apes—tarsiers lack opposable thumbs. But this does not hinder their climbing ability. Their long, spidery fingers are well adapted for the trees. Tarsiers also have special pads under each of their fingers and toes that help them to hang on to vertical tree trunks and bamboo stems in the forests.

Tarsiers are the only entirely carnivorous primate, feeding largely on arthropods such as grubs, ants, beetles, cockroaches, and scorpions. They also eat a wide variety of other small animals, including lizards and frogs.

Tarsiers are nocturnal animals with huge eyes and moveable ears. The oversized eyes let in more light, providing excellent night vision. And though the tarsier's eyes do not roll in their sockets as freely as ours, they are able to see all around themselves, thanks to their ability to turn their heads completely around much the way owls do.

Tarsiers live singly or in pairs and are highly territorial animals, constantly scent-marking their **territories** with urine to keep out competitors. While that works for other tarsiers, it does not keep out predators.

Eaten principally by owls, tarsiers also fall prey to small cats and other forest carnivores. But their natural enemies have not made the tarsier an endangered species. The pressure of growing human population and the increasing demand for timber and land in the Philippines are bringing them close to extinction.

Polar Bear

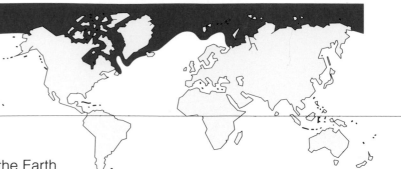

Ursus maritimus

Range: Arctic (north polar) regions around the Earth
Size: Shoulder height: 4–5 ft (1.21–1.52 m)
Weight: 600–1,340 lbs (272.16–607.82 kg)
Habitat: Arctic islands, coasts and ice floes
Food: Seals; may scavenge carcasses of whales or walruses and occasionally eat small mammals, birds, and eggs
Reproduction: Gestation: 6 months; mothers den up for the winter and generally have 1–3 very small cubs, about 1 lb (.45 kg) in weight
Life Span: 25–30 years
Threats: Poaching, pollution, human encroachment

Polar bears have many unique characteristics that help them stay warm through the Arctic winters. Their hollow hair insulates in the same way as a down coat or the insulation in your house—by trapping air, and keeping out the cold. And although their hair is white, polar bears' skin is black and can absorb heat from the sun which passes down through the bear's hollow hairs. In summer, when it is much warmer in the Arctic, some of this coat is shed.

Even the feet of the polar bear are special. It is the only bear with dense hair on the soles of its feet. This insulates them from the ice, and also provides traction. The forepaws are slightly webbed to aid in swimming.

Polar bears live only in the far northern areas of the Earth and are Arctic predators. Their principal prey are seals, though they will eat smaller animals when available. However, even though it is often depicted in cartoons, polar bears *never* eat penguins; all 17 species of penguins live only in the southern hemisphere.

Today polar bears are threatened by illegal hunting for trophies. Their remote habitat once protected them from poachers, but low-flying sea planes and helicopters have made it easy for humans to track them down and shoot them from great distances with high-powered rifles. Water pollution has also begun to affect the food chain that they depend upon in the north polar region.

Red Panda

Ailurus fulgens

Range: Himalayas to southern China
Size: Length (excluding tail): 16–24 in (40.64–60.96 cm)
Weight: 7–11 lbs (3.18–4.99 kg)
Habitat: Remote, high-altitude bamboo forests
Food: Bamboo, fruit, roots, acorns, lichens
Reproduction: Gestation: 90–140 days; 1–4 young are born each year (commonly 2)
Life Span: Up to 14 years
Threats: Human population growth, deforestation, agriculture

The red panda lives in bamboo forests high up on cool, steep ridges, where the local people call it *hun-ho*, meaning "fire fox." It is crepuscular—that is, most active during twilight hours, and sleeping in a tree during the day, safe from its natural enemies, the leopard and the bear.

It is somewhat territorial and solitary, traveling alone or in small family groups. While usually quiet, the panda does make sounds. A panda call is a series of short whistles or squeaks. If threatened, it may snort or hiss sharply.

The mother panda makes a den in a hollow tree or a rock crevice. Litters are small, with one or two young, which grow slowly. They stay with the mother for about a year, or until a new litter is about to be born.

The red panda was once thought to be a kind of cat, hence the scientific name *Ailurus fulgens*, or "shining cat." Even now scientists question whether the pandas belong in the raccoon family, the bear family, or their own separate family. As its name suggests, the red panda has been thought to be a close relative of the giant panda.

The highly specialized red panda is well adapted to life in a stable habitat. With a diet found only in limited areas, solitary lifestyle, and slow reproductive rate, it has thrived unchanged for 4.5 million years.

Now the habitat is changing, as cultivation destroys the bamboo forests. The pandas cannot adapt to the changes and so they are gradually disappearing. Conservationists hope that Chinese attempts to control human population growth will hold down the pressure to clear the bamboo forests.

Ruffed Lemur

Varecia variegata

Range: East coast rain forest of Madagascar
Size: Body length: up to 2 ft (.60 m); tail: up to 23 in (58.42 cm)
Weight: 8–11 lbs (3.63–4.99 kg)
Food: Fruit
Reproduction: Gestation: 4–5 months; high rate of twin births
Life Span: Up to 19 years in captivity; not known in the wild
Threats: Deforestation

Lemurs might be called the ghosts of Madagascar, for *lemur* is the Latin word for ghost. Lemurs are primitive primates found only on the island of Madagascar, today known as the Malagasy Republic. They have a habit of sunning themselves early in the morning, and because of this, they were once protected as holy sun worshippers embodying the souls of native ancestors. As the human population has increased, and old beliefs have faded, lemurs have lost this protection and are gravely endangered by destruction of 90 percent of Madagascar's forests.

Because Madagascar is an island, lemurs have evolved in many forms with little outside competition. The ruffed lemur is one of the larger species of lemurs. Its coat is so dense that it sheds water even during a heavy downpour, which is handy for life in the rain forest. The hair is also used to line the nest that the female makes for the young. Ruffed lemurs can be either black and white or black and red. The males and the females are usually about the same size. Like most lemurs, they are very active and agile as they leap through the trees, emitting frequent loud calls.

Like many mammals, lemurs have a much better sense of smell than we do. And they don't use it only to find plants to eat in the jungle. They mark branches of trees or even each other with their scents and use their sense of smell as a means of communication. Primatologists (scientists who study primate behavior) believe that the lemurs communicate different messages with different scents. Some scents protect a territory by keeping competing lemurs out, while other smells may be used to attract the attention of mates.

Lemurs use sound to communicate, too. In fact, ruffed lemurs can be one of the noisiest mammals in the world. They use loud calls to warn of possible dangers and to maintain spacing between groups.

Rusty-spotted Cat

Felis rubiginosus

Range: Southern India, Sri Lanka
Size: Length, excluding tail: 8–10 in (20.32–25.40 cm)
Weight: 2–4.5 lbs (.91–2.03 kg)
Habitat: Scrub and forest around waterways and human settlements
Food: Small mammals, birds, insects, reptiles
Reproduction: Gestation: 50–56 days; litter: 2–4 kittens
Life Span: 10–15 years
Threats: Human encroachment, habitat loss, poaching

The rusty-spotted cat is the smallest cat in the world. An adult is about one-half the size of a domestic house cat. But like all 37 species of cats, it is entirely carnivorous, hunting small mammals, birds, and lizards. This rare species is found only in two places, the arid scrubland of southern India and the humid forests of Sri Lanka. It hides during the day in trees or under bushes and hunts at night.

Like all cats, the rusty-spotted cat has excellent vision and relies primarily on its eyes in the hunt for prey. These nocturnal hunters have binocular vision, like our own: both eyes are on the front of their head, giving them better depth perception than that of animals with eyes on the sides of their head. Because their eyes are far more sensitive to light, rusty-spotted cats possess much better night vision than humans have.

Rusty-spotted cats suffer most from loss of habitat. The large and growing population in India leaves wildlife with less and less wild space. As a result, the cats are being crowded out of existence. This is true not only for predators like wild cats, but also for the entire living ecosystem of which they are a part. The pressure of increasing human population directly affects all levels of the food web, from producers (plants) to herbivores (mice) to carnivores (rusty-spotted cats).

Snow Leopard

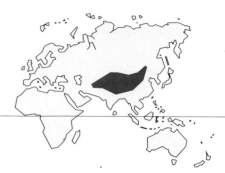

Panthera uncia

Range: The Himalayas and other mountains of Central Asia
Size: Shoulder height: 18–32 in (45.72–81.28 cm)
Weight: 88–165 lbs (39.92–74.85 kg)
Habitat: Mountain steppe and coniferous forest scrub at altitudes between 5,906–18,045 ft (1,800–5,500 m)
Food: Ibex, markhor, wild sheep, musk deer, marmots, hares
Reproduction: Gestation: 98–103 days; litter: 1–4
Life Span: Up to 15 years in captivity
Threats: Poaching; human encroachment

Snow leopards, as the name suggests, are perfectly adapted to life in the high altitudes of the mountains of Central Asia. Like all leopards, they have very long tails that help them to keep their balance when they leap. Their fur is among the thickest and longest of all cats, insulating them from the ice and snow. Their spots and uneven gray coloring allow them to blend into the mountains where they hunt and live. Even their feet help in the snow leopard's survival. Big, and furry on the bottom, they work like snowshoes, helping to keep the cats from sinking through the snow or slipping on the ice.

Snow leopards eat a wide variety of animals, but their principal prey are the wild goats and sheep which coexist with them in the mountains and forests of Mongolia, China, Afghanistan, Russia, Pakistan, India, Nepal, and Bhutan. Snow leopards are famous for leaping great distances in pursuit of a meal, sometimes as far as 25 feet (7.62 m). But like most hunters they tend to be patient and quiet, preferring to wait until their prey is closer to give them a better chance of capture.

Field biologists also need to be patient and quiet when studying animals in the wild. This is especially true with snow leopards because they are extremely elusive animals, only recently tracked with the use of **radio telemetry**. This research has revealed that snow leopards are often most active in the early morning and twilight hours and that their home range covers an area up to about 15 square miles (39 sq km).

Like most of the spotted or striped cats of the world, the snow leopard is hunted for its beautiful fur. Although it is now illegal to hunt them or to sell products made from their skin, snow leopard fur coats are still available in China.

Sumatran Rhino

Dicerorhinus sumatrensis

Range: Southeast Asia, Sumatra, Borneo
Size: Shoulder height: 3.5–4.5 ft (1.07–1.37 m)
Weight: 1,000–2,000 lbs (907.2–1814.4 kg)
Habitat: Montane rain forests
Food: Short grasses, woody browse, sapling ends, shoots, fruits
Life Span: 32 years
Reproduction: Gestation: unknown; 1 calf per birth
Main Threat: Poaching, habitat loss

The Sumatran rhino has the distinction of being the smallest and oldest surviving species of rhino, as well as the first type of rhino ever born in captivity—at the Calcutta Zoo in 1889. Sometimes called "the hairy rhino" for its bristly hair, it is a relic of ice-age ancestors, the wooly rhinos that lived 50,000 to 100,000 years ago.

The bigger African rhinos live on open grasslands, but the Sumatran rhino is suited to life in the rain forest. Their smaller stature makes it possible for them to move freely through the forest foraging for leaves, grasses, and a wide variety of plants.

Unfortunately, as the jungle disappears, so does the Sumatran rhino. It is one of the most endangered of all rhinos, and the few hundred animals left have no place to go in a rapidly shrinking habitat.

For centuries, all five species of rhinoceros (Indian, black, white, Sumatran, Javan) have been both admired and hunted. Today they are *all* endangered species. To save them from extinction will take international cooperation by conservationists, animal traders, law enforcement officers, native people, and many others. And zoos play an important role, too. Through the American Association of Zoological Parks and Aquariums' conservation and breeding program—the Species Survival Plan (SSP), zoos are cooperating to breed and keep rhinos safe in a sort of "modern-day ark" until rhino preserves are safe enough from poachers so that populations again can increase in the wild.

The Indonesian government and several American zoos have agreed to work to increase captive breeding of the Sumatran rhino. The first captive pair of this species in the United States in recent history was placed at the the Cincinnati Zoo in 1991. Plans for additional breeding groups are being established at three other zoos in North America and Indonesia.

Tiger

Panthera tigris

Range: India, Nepal, Manchuria, China, S.E. Asia and Indonesia

Size: Average shoulder height: 3 ft (.91 m); length, including tail, depending on sub-species: 7–12 ft (2.13–3.65 m)

Weight: 250–700 lbs (113.4–317.52 kg)

Habitat: Varied by sub-species; includes tropical rain forest, coniferous and deciduous forests, mangrove swamps and drier forests

Food: Deer, antelope, monkeys, and birds; preferred prey is hoofed animals

Reproduction: Gestation: 100–105 days; litter: 2–4 cubs, each about 2 lbs (.91 kg)

Life Span: 15 years; 20 in captivity

Threats: Habitat destruction, human encroachment

Tigers are the largest cats in the world and have a very wide range, so it is surprising that they are endangered throughout their native range. While they do not all look alike, all tigers are the same species. Different subspecies of tigers come from different parts of Asia.

The Siberian tiger lives the farthest north and is the largest of all tigers, weighing up to 700 pounds (317.52 kg) and growing as long as 12 feet (3.65 m), including the tail. Its thick, shaggy coat is generally lighter in color than that of tigers living farther south.

The Indo-Chinese tiger (small photo) from tropical forests of Southeast Asia and Malaysia is a darker, brownish orange color, which helps it to blend into the jungle. Tigers need heavy plant growth to conceal their approach to prey. But defoliants used during the Vietnam War destroyed this cover, and the Indo-Chinese tiger has never recovered.

The most famous tigers, Bengal tigers from India (large photo), are medium-sized, weigh 400 to 500 pounds (181.44 to 226.80 kg) and stand 3 to 4 feet (.91 to 1.21 m) at the shoulder. They can reach 9 feet (2.74 m) in length, including a 3-foot-long tail.

Since 1972 the World Wildlife Fund has cooperated with the Indian government in a project called "Operation Tiger," helping to establish protected reserves and working with local people to help them live with tigers. As a result, over the past 20 years, the number of Bengal tigers in the wild has doubled, from 2,000 to over 4,000, according to Indian wildlife officials.

Walrus

Odobenus rosmarus

Range: Arctic seas, from eastern Canada and Greenland to Alaska
Size: Length: 8–15 ft (2.43–4.57 m)
Weight: 1,800–4,900 lbs (816.48–2,222.64 kg)
Habitat: Chiefly, seasonal pack ice over continental shelf
Food: Principally mollusks
Reproduction: Gestation: 15–16 months (including 4–5 months of suspended development due to delayed implantation); one offspring every 2–3 years
Life Span: Up to 40 years
Threats: Poaching (for tusks)

Walruses live only in arctic waters of the far north, but there are two different populations—one in the Pacific Ocean and the other in the Atlantic Ocean.

Walruses have about 450 coarse whiskers—called vibrissae—on their snouts. These whiskers are very sensitive and are used to find food in dark water. A walrus can even use its whiskers to move food off the sea bottom and into its mouth.

Walruses blush to keep their cool, not when they lose it. The skin becomes filled with blood so heat can be released from the surface. This makes the walrus's skin redder than usual. They automatically adjust their blood flow to the surface of their skin to survive a life of extreme temperatures. In the very cold weather of the Arctic Circle, walruses retain body heat by reducing the flow of blood to their skin.

For many hundreds of years native peoples hunted walruses for food, clothing, and shelter, generally never killing more than they needed. So hunting did not endanger the walrus population. But European and North American hunters began killing walruses for commercial uses in the early seventeenth century, primarily for the ivory tusks. Like whales, walruses were also hunted for blubber that is used to make oil. Because of overhunting, the world walrus population was decimated by the early 1900s.

The United States Marine Mammal Protection Act, which prohibits the import and sale of walrus products, has helped the species make a comeback. The Pacific population has increased from 100,000 in 1950 to 237,000 in 1991. The Atlantic population, although not as plentiful, has increased to 25,000. Today, only Alaskan natives who have traditionally depended on the walrus for food and clothing are allowed to continue to hunt them, on a very limited basis.

White-cheeked Gibbon

Hylobates concolor

Range: Laos, Vietnam, South China
Size of Animal: Length: 14–22 in (35.36–55.88 cm)
Weight: 9–12 lbs (4.08–5.45 kg)
Habitat: Evergreen rain forests and semideciduous monsoon forests
Food: Leaves, fruits
Reproduction: Gestation: 7–8 months; single offspring every 2–3 years
Life Span: To 25 years
Threats: Human encroachment, destruction of rain forests

At first glance, male and female white-cheeked gibbons appear to be different species. The female is golden and the male is black and has the white cheek patches that give this species its name. This small ape is among the most agile of all animals in the trees, where it spends most of its life.

Gibbons travel in small family groups, foraging for fruits in treetops. They are highly territorial, defending their feeding area even from other types of animals. To warn away other feeding groups, both the male and the female produce loud hooting calls that carry for great distances. Gibbons are among the loudest and most vocal of all mammals.

Because of their small size, some people mistakenly think gibbons are monkeys, rather than apes. The gibbon is considered a lesser ape, while the gorilla, orangutan, and chimpanzee are great apes. The main differences between monkeys and apes is that apes do not have tails and walk upright or semi-erect, supported by their elongated arms.

The gibbon's slight body, flexible shoulders, and long arms and hands allow it to swing through the trees in a hand-over-hand manner. A gibbon's circulatory system is different from ours and enables it to hang from its hands for hours. A relaxed gibbon moves at the speed of a walking person, but if frightened or excited it can move amazingly fast, even leaping 20 feet (6.10 m) or more with ease.

The rain forests of Southeast Asia are under pressure from human encroachment, making the white-cheeked gibbon an endangered species. Large preserves are needed for the survival of these and other mammals in this part of the world.

The list of endangered mammals does not end here.
There are many more, including the three shown on this page.
The challenge, and the hope, is to rescue these animals
and to protect others from becoming endangered.

Giant Kangaroo Rat
Dipodomys ingens

Range: California
Size: 14 in (35.56 cm) long
Weight: 6.4 oz (181.44 g)
Habitat: Dry, open grassland
Food: Seeds, new plant growth
Reproduction: Gestation: about 1 month; litter: 2–4
Life Span: 5–6 years
Threats: Poisoning, loss of food and living areas

Indiana Bat
Myotis sodalis

Range: Indiana, Missouri, Kentucky
Size: 3 in (7.62 cm) long;
8–9 in (20.32–22.86 cm) wingspan
Weight: .06 oz (1.5 g)
Habitat: Cool caves
Food: Moths and other flying insects
Reproduction: Gestation: 50–60 days;
single young per season
Life Span: 4–6 years
Threats: Human disturbance during
hibernation; deforestation

Humpback Whale
Megaptera novaeangliae

Range: Oceanic; polar to tropical seas
Size: Body length: 75–90 ft (22.86–27.43 m)
Weight: 25–45 tons (22,680–40,824 kg)
Habitat: Open ocean, sometimes coastal areas
Food: Schooling fish, crustaceans, plankton
Reproduction: Gestation: 11–12 months;
one calf every 2–3 years
Life Span: 95 years, estimated
Main Threat: Human predation

Glossary

arboreal   living in trees

baleen   filters made of keratin in the mouths of some whales; sometimes called whalebone

captivity   the state of being confined, as when an animal is kept in a zoo

carnivore   an animal that eats other animals

ecology   the study of the interrelationships between living things and their environment

ecosystem   a community of living things and its environment

endangered species   a species whose numbers have been reduced to the point of nearly disappearing

environment   the living and nonliving characteristics of a region, including air, water, land and living organisms

extinct   no longer in existence

gestation   the time from fertilization to birth, often called pregnancy in human beings

habitat   the area and physical conditions where an animal or plant lives in the wild

herbivore   animals, such as hoofed animals and rodents, that eat plants

insectivore   animals, such as shrews, hedgehogs, and North American bats, that principally eat insects

litter   the offspring produced at one time by a mammal

omnivore   animals that eat plants and animals, such as raccoons and humans

pesticide   a chemical used to kill species regarded as pests

poaching   illegal hunting of a species

pollution   the introduction of harmful, or over-abundant, substances into the environment

population   a group of the same species living in a given area

predator   an animal that hunts and kills other animals for food

prey   an animal hunted by other animals for food

radio telemetry   a method of remote tracking used by field biologists to chart the movement of a wild animal species

species   a specific kind of plant or animal which can mate and produce young like themselves

range   the wild area in which a species is found

temperate   the Earth's regions between the equatorial tropical regions and the polar regions

territory   the area defended and controlled against intrusion by individuals of the same species

threatened   facing serious threats to survival in the wild; nearly endangered status

tropical rain forest   very dense equatorial forest constituting the most diverse ecosystem on earth, home to more than half of all plant and animal species; characterized by warm temperatures, high rainfall, and tall broad-leaved trees that remain green all year

vertebrate   an animal with a segmented bony spinal column. The group of vertebrates includes mammals, birds, reptiles, amphibians and fish

Conservation Organizations

Center for Reproduction of Endangered Wildlife
Cincinnati Zoo & Botanical Garden
3400 Vine St.
Cincinnati, OH 45220

Conservation International
1015 18th St., NW
Suite 1000
Washington, DC 20036

Cousteau Society
930 W. 21st Street
Norfolk, VA 23517

Greenpeace, USA
1436 U St., NW
Washington, DC 20039

National Audubon Society
950 Third Ave.
New York, NY 10022

The Nature Conservancy
1815 N. Lynn Street
Arlington, VA 22209

National Wildlife Federation
1400 16th St., NW
Washington, DC 20036

Rain Forest Action Network
301 Broadway, Suite A
San Francisco, CA 94133

The Sierra Club
730 Polk St.
San Francisco, CA 94109

Wildlife Conservation International
New York Zoological Society
185th St. & Southern Blvd.
Bronx, NY 10460

Wildlife Preservation Trust International
34th St. & Girard Ave.
Philadelphia, PA 19104

The Wilderness Society
900 17th St., NW
Washington, DC 20036

World Wildlife Fund
1250 24th St., NW
Washington, DC 20037

Further Reading

Burton, Maurice, ed. *The Funk & Wagnalls Wildlife Encyclopedia.* New York: Funk & Wagnalls, 1970.

Chinery, Michael. *The Complete Amateur Naturalist.* New York: Crescent Books, 1977.

Huxley, Julian, ed. *The Atlas of World Wildlife.* New York: Rand McNally, 1973.

Lampton, Christopher. *Endangered Species.* New York: Franklin Watts, 1988.

Rinard, Judith. *Wildlife: Making a Comeback.* Washington, DC: National Geographic Society Books, 1987.

Scheffel, Richard L. *The ABC's of Nature.* New York: Reader's Digest Books, 1984.

Stuart, Gene S. *Wildlife Alert! The Struggle to Survive.* Washington, DC: National Geographic Society Books, 1980.

Whitfield, Philip. *Can the Whales Be Saved?* New York: Viking Kestrel, 1989.

Williams, John, G. *A Field Guide to the National Parks of East Africa.* London: Collins, 1986.

PERIODICALS

Audubon magazine

International Wildlife magazine

National Wildlife magazine

Ranger Rick magazine

Wildlife Conservation magazine

ZOOBOOKS, 930 W. Washington Street, San Diego, CA 92103 (published monthly)

Index

Walrus

Gray Wolf

Polar Bear

Indiana Bat

Humpback Whale

Black-footed Ferret

Giant Kangaroo Rat

Jaguar

Cotton-top Tamarin

Gorilla

Okapi

Black Rhinoceros

African Elephant

Ruffed Lemur